Mad about...

Whales and Dolphins

written by Anita Ganeri
illustrated by Sue Hendra and Paul Linnet

consultant: The Whale and Dolphin Conservation Society
www.wdcs.org

A catalogue record for this book is available from the British Library

Published by Ladybird Books Ltd
80 Strand London WC2R 0RL
A Penguin Company

2 4 6 8 10 9 7 5 3 1
© LADYBIRD BOOKS LTD MMVIII. This edition MMXII

ISBN: 978-0-71819-597-7

Printed in China

Contents

Some words appear in **bold** in this book.
Turn to the glossary to learn about them.

What are whales and dolphins?

Whales and dolphins look similar to fish, but they are **mammals**, just like us. They have to come to the surface to breathe, even though they live in the sea. They look after their babies when they are born, and feed them on milk.

There are about 85 types of whales and dolphins. They live in oceans all around the world.

The Gulf of California porpoise, or vaquita, is only about 1.35 metres long

Whales, dolphins and porpoises come in all sorts of shapes, colours and sizes, but they have features that help to tell them apart. For example, a dolphin has a long snout, called a 'beak', and a porpoise has a blunt head with no beak.

porpoise

dolphin

The white bands on this minke whale's flippers show that it lives in the northern oceans

Bottlenose dolphins sometimes leap out of the sea, using a flick of their powerful tails

7

Body bits

Whales and dolphins have bodies that are perfectly suited for life in the sea. They have many special features to help them swim, find food, keep warm and breathe.

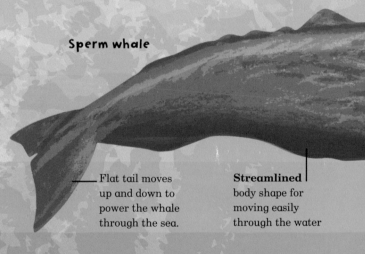

Sperm whale

Flat tail moves up and down to power the whale through the sea.

Streamlined body shape for moving easily through the water

The **ancestors** of today's whales once lived on land. About 50 million years ago, they moved into the sea and their bodies changed. Their front legs became flippers for swimming and their nostrils became **blowholes** on top of their heads.

Toothed whales have one blowhole, but **baleen** whales have two.

Blowhole for breathing

The whale uses its flippers for turning, steering and balancing

Blubber under the whale's skin keeps it warm

Sperm whales only have teeth in their bottom jaws

If you have a computer, you can download posters of different whales and dolphins from www.ladybird.com/madabout

9

Teeth and feeding

Whales can be split into two groups. Some whales have teeth and are called 'toothed whales'. Some have no teeth. They are called 'baleen whales'. These types of whales catch food and eat in different ways.

Toothed whales such as sperm whales, and dolphins such as orcas have sharp, peg-like teeth for grabbing food. They usually eat fish and squid, although orcas also hunt other sea mammals, such as seals and sealions.

Orca

Baleen whales, such as blue whales and humpback whales, eat tiny sea creatures. Instead of teeth, these whales have bristly brushes (baleen plates) hanging down inside their mouths. The whale gulps in water, then pushes the water out again through its baleen plates. The baleen plates work like a sieve, trapping the food.

Humpback whale

A humpback whale blows bubbles to help it catch its food. The bubbles make a net around a **shoal** of fish, trapping them inside. Then the whale swims up through the middle and gulps down its meal.

11

Wonderful whales

The blue whale is the largest sea mammal and the biggest animal that has ever lived. An adult whale can weigh as much as twenty African elephants.

Right whales swim near the ocean surface, skimming their mouths over the water to collect food.

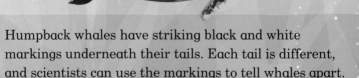

Humpback whales have striking black and white markings underneath their tails. Each tail is different, and scientists can use the markings to tell whales apart.

The bodies of Cuvier's beaked whales
are often covered in tiny scars.
It is thought that these scars
are from being bitten by
cookie-cutter sharks!

Bottlenose whales are easy to recognize by
their bulging foreheads and bottle-shaped
snouts. They feed in very deep water and
can hold their breath for about an hour
when they dive.

A sperm whale's huge head takes up a third of its
body and is bigger than a car. It is filled with oily
wax that scientists think may help the whale to dive.

Delightful dolphins

Dall's porpoises have short, thick bodies and small heads. They are fast swimmers, zigzagging through the water at high speed.

White-sided dolphins are large dolphins that grow up to 2.8 metres long. They are easy to recognize by the white stripes and yellow patches on their sides.

The Hector's dolphin is only about 1.4 metres long and is one of the smallest dolphins. It likes to leap out of the water and land on its side with a big splash!

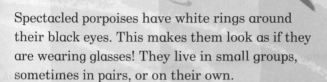

Spectacled porpoises have white rings around
their black eyes. This makes them look as if they
are wearing glasses! They live in small groups,
sometimes in pairs, or on their own.

Although orcas
are sometimes called
killer whales, they are
actually the largest
type of dolphin. They have
the tallest **dorsal fins** of all
whales, up to 1.8 metres tall. That's
about the same size as a grown man.

Bottlenose dolphins
are dark grey on top
and light grey or white underneath.
This makes them difficult to see, both
above the surface and from below.

15

The weird and wonderful!

Most types of whales and dolphins look alike and share the same body shape. But some have strange and unusual features that make them easy to recognize.

Belugas live in the Arctic Ocean. Baby belugas are brownish-grey but get lighter as they get older. By the age of six, they are yellowish-white in colour.

Male narwhals have a twisted **tusk** that grows up to 3 metres long. Males use their tusks to fight each other for females.

The Ganges river dolphin has a long, pointed snout, filled with more than one hundred sharp teeth. Short hairs on its snout help it to find food in the muddy water.

Spinner dolphins are
champion acrobats.
They love to leap out of
the water and spin around
and around. They can spin up
to seven times in a single leap!

Risso's dolphins are easy to recognize by the white scars on their skin. These scars are caused by fighting and playing with other Risso's dolphins.

17

On the move

Some whales make long journeys every year. This is called migrating. The whales travel to places where they can find food, or find a **mate** and have babies.

In summer, grey whales feed in the Arctic Ocean. Then they swim down the west coast of North America to Mexico, where they **breed**.

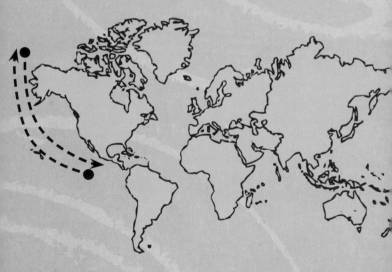

The next spring, they head back north. This is a round trip of more than 20,000 kilometres and the longest journey made by a mammal.

Narwhals are found in the icy Arctic Ocean. In summer, they live close to the coast. In winter, as the ocean freezes over, they migrate away from the shore so they don't get trapped by ice.

Like grey whales, humpback whales travel huge distances every year. They feed in the cold seas close to the North and South poles, then move to warmer waters to mate and breed. On their migration, they may go for many months without food.

Talking underwater

Whales and dolphins can use sounds and songs to 'talk' to each other underwater. Some of them also have a special way of using sound to hunt for food and find their way around.

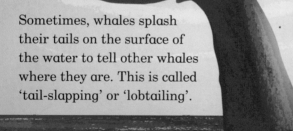

Sometimes, whales splash their tails on the surface of the water to tell other whales where they are. This is called 'tail-slapping' or 'lobtailing'.

Male humpback whales sing songs to females. Each song lasts for about half an hour and may be sung over and over again.

Belugas are nicknamed 'sea canaries' because they chirp and whistle like birds. They can also pull different faces but no one is sure what these mean.

Some whales, especially humpbacks and orcas, like to poke their heads above the surface of the water to see what is going on. This is called 'spyhopping'.

Dolphins make clicking noises that hit objects in the water and send back echoes. The dolphins listen to the echoes to decide which way to swim. This is called **echolocation**.

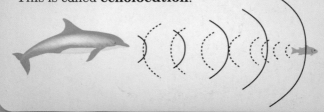

Family life

Many whales and dolphins live in large families called **pods**, or **schools**. Dolphins are known to live in groups of many hundreds. They help each other to find food and defend themselves.

Giving birth

1. A baby whale is born underwater, tail first.

2. Its mother pushes it to the surface so that it can take its first breath.

3. The baby can swim straight away.

A baby whale or dolphin is called a **calf**. The calf stays with its mother for two to three years. At first, it feeds on its mother's milk. Later, she teaches it how to find food. She also guards it from enemies, such as sharks and orcas.

Sperm whale mothers live together in groups with their calves. There are also females without calves, called 'aunts'. When the mothers go to find food, the aunts take care of the babies.

Save the whale!

People used to hunt whales for their meat, oil and baleen. They killed so many that some types of whale nearly died out. Today, whales and dolphins are still in danger. Some are killed by **pollution**. Others get trapped in fishing nets and eventually drown.

Each year, thousands of dolphins die when they get caught in fishing nets. They cannot reach the surface to breathe. Look out for dolphin-friendly tuna. This tuna is fished with a rod and line so no dolphins get hurt.

The Yangtze river dolphin from China became **extinct** in 2007. It died out because so many dolphins got caught in fishing nets or hit by boats, had their **habitat** destroyed, or were poisoned by pollution.

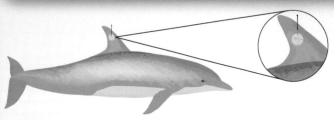

Scientists work hard to learn more about whales and dolphins. Some use special tags that are carefully attached to dolphins' fins. Scientists then follow signals from the tags to see how the dolphins behave in the wild.

In some countries, people can go whale and dolphin watching on boats. This allows them to see these amazing animals up close in their natural habitat without harming them.

25

Fantastic facts

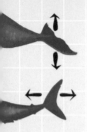

- The best way to tell a whale from a fish is by its tail. Whales have **horizontal** tails that they move up and down as they swim. Fish have **vertical** tails that they move from side to side.

- If you open your eyes in the sea, the salt can make them sting. So whales and dolphins make special oily tears to protect their eyes.

- The bowhead whale has the thickest blubber of any animal. The blubber can be 50 centimetres thick. That's as thick as a pile of fifty of these books.

- Dolphins do not chew their food, but swallow it whole. They only use their teeth for grabbing hold of prey.

- The sperm whale has the biggest brain of any animal. Its brain weighs about 7.8 kilograms, about five times as much as a human brain.

whale brain   **human brain**

- In the wild, dolphins can live to be at least fifty years old.

- Whales and dolphins never really go to sleep, as we do. They just rest half their brains at a time, when floating on the sea surface or swimming.

- Blue whales are so enormous that they could not live on land. The weight of their bodies would crush their lungs so they wouldn't be able to breathe.

- People used to believe that narwhal tusks were actually unicorn horns. The horns were sold for a lot of money and so many narwhals were killed that they almost became extinct.

- The long-snouted spinner dolphin has up to 250 teeth.

- Some whales have tiny creatures, called whale lice, living and feeding on their skin. A single whale may be home to as many as 100,000 lice!

Amazing awards

Fastest

The orca can reach a top speed
of 55 kilometres per hour.
That's almost six times quicker
than the fastest human swimmer.

Biggest

A blue whale can weigh up to
190 tonnes and is about as
long as three buses. Its eyes
are as big as footballs and its
heart is the size of a car.

Deepest diver

A sperm whale can dive
down more than 3,000 metres
(nearly 2 miles) to find food.
It has to hold its breath for
almost two hours!

Loudest

Fin whales have voices that are louder than jet planes. They can be heard by other whales hundreds of kilometres away. However, their voices are too low for humans to hear.

Biggest baby

A newborn blue whale calf can measure up to 8 metres long. That's as long as four tall men laid down head to toe.

Smallest

The smallest dolphin is the vaquita porpoise. It grows to less than 1.5 metres long. Because of its small size it often gets caught in fishing nets and is in danger of becoming extinct.

Glossary

ancestor – a relative that lived a long time ago.

baleen – a type of whale that has bristly brushes hanging down in its mouth instead of teeth. These sieve food from the water.

blowhole – a hole on top of a whale's head through which the whale breathes, like a nostril.

blubber – a layer of fat under a whale's skin that helps to keep it warm in the cold sea.

breed – to produce offspring.

calf – a baby whale or dolphin.

dorsal fin – the fin on top of a whale's back.

echolocation – a way of locating objects and finding the way around by using sound.

extinct – to have died out.

habitat – the natural home of a plant or animal.

horizontal – lying flat in the sea or to the ground.

mammal – animals that give birth to live young and feed their babies on milk.

mate – an animal that another animal has babies with.

pod – a large group of whales or dolphins.

pollution – the way in which the seas and other places are being made dirty by dangerous liquids, oil and litter.

school – a large group of whales or dolphins.

shoal – a large group of fish.

streamlined – a long, slim body shape that can move easily through the water.

tusk – an extra-long pointed tooth.

vertical – standing upright in the sea or to the ground.